HOW TO
PRAY
FOR SOMEONE WHO HURT YOU

Crystal McGowen

HOW TO
PRAY
FOR SOMEONE WHO HURT YOU

TABLE OF CONTENTS

A NOTE FROM THE AUTHOR

You know what? I like you already, and I have a feeling that you and I would be good friends. I can imagine it... the two of us chatting over coffee, each of us sharing our struggles and rejoicing over victories together. How can I know this? Something tells me we're kindred spirits because not everyone wants to pray for their perceived (or real) enemies. Not everyone would turn to prayer when their heart feels broken and trampled upon. But you? You get it. You get that prayer is not a passive thing to do as a last resort. You know that prayer is the only way some things change.   And that's exactly what you want, change. I know, because I've been there too. Relationships are messy, expectations aren't met, and feelings get hurt. Life is full of broken promises, missed opportunities, and failures of all kinds.   Yet despite all of this, our souls are thirsty for acceptance, understanding, and love.

We desire to see change in our own hearts and minds, in our relationships, and in our spiritual lives, but how do we pursue this kind of change with wounded hearts? The answer is simple. Prayer.

In its most basic form, prayer is conversation between the Father, and his children.   Prayer requires the humble acknowledgement that God is the ultimate authority, and that we are in need of him. Sure, we need His guidance, His direction, and His counsel, but what we need most of all is *His presence*.

It is in the Presence of God that we are able to put on the 'mind of Christ' (1 Corinthians 2:16) and be able to respond to the brokenness around us with humility and compassion. And, this my friend, is what it's all about.

We cannot ask God to change in others what we are

unwilling to change in ourselves.

Praying for someone who has hurt you requires great humility, patience, and generosity of heart. Yet before I go much further into the 'how' of praying for someone who hurt you, I need to share a little secret with you. Well, maybe it's not quite a secret (because Jesus says it quite plainly in Matthew 7:1-5 below) but, it might change the way you think about praying for your offender. Consider these words of Jesus:

> Do not judge, or you too will be judged. For in the same way you judge others, you will be judged, and with the measure you use, it will be measured to you. "Why do you look at the speck of sawdust in your brother's eye and pay no attention to the plank in your own eye? How can you say to your brother, 'Let me take the speck out of your eye,' when all the time

there is a plank in your own eye? You hypocrite, first take the plank out of your own eye, and then you will see clearly to remove the speck from your brother's eye.

This is the 'secret' to praying for those who have hurt you, to pray for them like you would pray for yourself. With Matthew 7 in mind, I've written these prayers to be said collectively, over both you and your offender. I do this because both you and your offender are made in the image of God, and both you and your offender need grace. 2 Corinthians 5:14, 21 tells us that "one man died for everyone. That puts everyone in the same boat. He included everyone in his death so that everyone could also be included in his life, a resurrection life, a far better life than people ever lived on their own. How? You ask? In Christ. God put the wrong on him who never did anything wrong, so we could be put right with God" (The Message).

When we pray and put ourselves in 'the same boat' as our offenders, we're much less likely to throw stones, and beautiful things begin to happen in our own souls.

This is not the kind of prayer guide that will help you 'pray your way' to being right and somehow prove your offender to be wrong. If you are looking for Biblical justification to judge, discredit, or punish your offender, you are in the wrong place.

However, if you are looking for a guide to help you pray for your offender in such a way that God's presence is ushered in and welcomed in your life and in the life of your offender, then settle in and make yourself at home here. It is my hope that this guide will inspire you, bless you, and encourage you to pray over the difficult relationships in your life.

Praying with you,

Crystal

HOW TO USE THIS PRAYER GUIDE

The prayers offered here are written within the context of relationships in conflict and not all may apply to your unique situation. Feel free to adapt these prayers to each individual relationship in your life. While the prayers are numbered, there is no particular order to them. You can choose to pray one day at a time or choose to pray over the topic that you feel most drawn to.

There are numerous resources available online to assist with general prayer structure, however, this guide focuses purely on intercession. You are encouraged to also include praise, gratitude, prayers of lament, etc. in your prayers.

To begin:

- o Quiet yourself and invite the Holy Spirit to lead and guide your time of prayer.

- o Read the verse provided for each day at least once. You may want to re-read the passage and take note of which phrases or words stand out to you, and which phrases raise concerns or questions.

- o When you're ready to move on, read the verse-inspired prayer over you and your offender. For each "_____" that you see, insert your offender's name. It's okay if you're not ready to pray each prayer just yet. You may want to spend several days on one topic before moving on to the next, and you may need to pass over some topics until a later date. The important thing is that you keep praying and go at the pace that you feel led to pray.

- o Each day comes with a journaling page where you can write out your own prayer response for each topic.

The prayers provided here are short prayer starters, designed to provide you with a simple way to begin. Allow God to direct your prayers, being sensitive to His leading along the way.

While the Word of God is all powerful, the prayers listed here have no power or authority on their own. They are simply a first step when you're feeling broken and don't know where to start.

Ready?

Let us pray.

A PRAYER OF FORGIVENESS

Father,

You are holy and wise, and I come to you knowing that you care for my heart and know how to heal all of its brokenness. I know that you have called me to forgive from the heart, and that is what I desire to do. As I begin this prayer journey, would you reveal to me the ways that I have been selfish and unkind. Show me the error of my own ways, that I may repent of them and walk in your forgiveness.

Give me the ability to rest in your presence and fill me up with your love so that I can navigate this relationship that is so burdensome. While I realize that forgiveness is a journey, I commit myself to this path, knowing that you will gently lead me each step of the way until I am at peace. Show me how to forgive my offenders for each hurtful word and action and remove any bitter root in me.

I open my hands and I open my heart to receive your guidance. Lead me in ways of peace, love, and compassion. Show me how to bless those who have wounded me and show me how to forgive those who have offended me. May the words of my mouth and the meditations of my heart be pleasing in your sight, O God.

Amen.

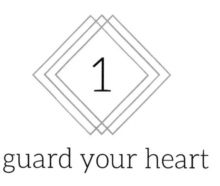

guard your heart

Proverbs 4:23-27

Above all else, guard your heart, for everything you do flows from it. Keep your mouth free of perversity; keep corrupt talk far from your lips. Let your eyes look straight ahead; fix your gaze directly before you. Give careful thought to the paths for your feet and be steadfast in all your ways. Do not turn to the right or the left; keep your foot from evil.

Lord Jesus, as I walk through this difficult season, would you help ___ and me to guard our hearts. Would we be sensitive to your leading, and sensitive to the ways the enemy would seek to tear us farther apart. Keep our mouths pure and clean, free from gossip and slander, free from complaining and arguing, and free from degrading and demeaning conversations. Fix our eyes straight ahead on you, keeping us mindful of the cross. Help us to think carefully about the words we say and the actions we take, not making hasty knee-jerk reactions, but instead, thoughtful, calculated, and prayerful responses. Help us not to sway from the guidance of your word and protect us in every way with your truth.

peace

Hebrews 12:14-15

Make every effort to live in peace with everyone and to be holy; without holiness no one will see the Lord. See to it that no one falls short of the grace of God and that no bitter root grows up to cause trouble and defile many.

Lord, I know that you have called us to peace. Guide ____ and me as we try to make amends. Would you speak to both of us, leading us in ways that are peaceful, showing us what to say and what to do. Help us to trust you, and to respond to each other in ways that are honoring. Use this conflict to show ____ and I what it means to walk in holiness. I know that without holiness my ability to see you will be hindered, so I give you permission to pull up any bitter root in me. Give me discernment so that I will never tolerate bitterness or resentment in my heart. May I live out a testimony of grace so that others see your goodness in my life.

3

vision

Ephesians 1:17-19, The Message

I couldn't stop thanking God for you—every time I prayed, I'd think of you and give thanks. But I do more than thank. I ask—ask the God of our Master, Jesus Christ, the God of glory—to make you intelligent and discerning in knowing him personally, your eyes focused and clear, so that you can see exactly what it is he is calling you to do, grasp the immensity of this glorious way of life he has for his followers, oh, the utter extravagance of his work in us who trust him—endless energy, boundless strength!

Father, thank you for _____. Thank you for making both of us in your image and for loving us relentlessly. Because of this great love, I ask that you give _____ wisdom and discernment in knowing you. And I pray that you would give me wisdom and discernment as well. Give us a Kingdom-clear vision so that we will know exactly what your will is and what you have called us to do. Would you help _____ understand the abundant life you have called her/him to, and would you let us lean on your strength as we grow in our ability to trust you.

4

blameless

Philippians 1:9-11

And this is my prayer: that your love may abound more and more in knowledge and depth of insight, so that you may be able to discern what is best and may be pure and blameless for the day of Christ, filled with the fruit of righteousness that comes through Jesus Christ—to the glory and praise of God.

Lord Jesus, this is my prayer for _____ and for myself. Fill us with your love. May we grow in the knowledge of how to love you and how to love each other. Strip away any falsehoods that we may believe and give us the ability to discern what is best and pure. Give us blameless hearts. Each day as we move forward, would we be able to end the day without regrets, knowing that we have acted in love and can stand before you blameless. Give us righteous lives and may you be glorified as a result.

5

strength

Ephesians 3:16-21

I pray that out of his glorious riches he may strengthen you with power through his Spirit in your inner being, so that Christ may dwell in your hearts through faith. And I pray that you, being rooted and established in love, may have power, together with all the saints, to grasp how wide and long and high and deep is the love of Christ, and to know this love that surpasses knowledge-that you may be filled to the measure of all the fullness of God. Now to him who can do immeasurably more than all we ask or imagine, according to his power that is at work within us, to him be glory...

Lord Jesus, you have strength enough for all of us, and today I pray that this strength would rest on _____. Rest on me too. Grow our faith and understanding of who you are, showing us your fullness and great love. May _____ and I be deeply rooted in you, and would we find satisfaction and wholeness in your love. Give us the ability to fully understand how deep and high and wide your love is for us. Lord, overwhelm _____ and I with your love right now. May it sink deep into our hearts and minds until we are filled up with you. Lord, you can do more than all I can ever imagine, and I ask that you let your love be felt, known, and accepted in the life of _____ today.

mindset

1 Corinthians 2:12, 16

What we have received is not the spirit of the world, but the Spirit who is from God, so that we may understand what God has freely given us... But we have the mind of Christ.

Lord Jesus, in every way, may _____ and I reject the spirit and wisdom of this world. May we rest exclusively in you. May we cling to what is good and flee from what is evil. Clear our minds from the world's jargon and enable our minds to focus on the truth of your word. Give us the ability to grasp how deeply you love us, and how great your forgiveness is. Help us not to dwell on what is offensive, but may your minds dwell on whatever is true, whatever is noble, whatever is right, whatever is pure, whatever is lovely, whatever is admirable - if anything is excellent or praiseworthy - may we think about such things. (Philippians 4:6) Give us your mind that we might hear your voice and give me your heart for _____.

7

knowledge

Colossians 1:9-14

We continually ask God to fill you with the knowledge of his will through all the wisdom and understanding that the Spirit gives, so that you may live a life worthy of the Lord and please him in every way: bearing fruit in every good work, growing in the knowledge of God, being strengthened with all power according to his glorious might so that you may have great endurance and patience, and giving joyful thanks to the Father, who has qualified you to share in the inheritance of his holy people in the kingdom of light. For he has rescued us from the dominion of darkness and brought us into the kingdom of the Son he loves, in whom we have redemption, the forgiveness of sins.

Father, it is humbling that you have forgiven and qualified me for your inheritance. Help me wrap my mind around this, fully embracing that by your grace you call me 'holy.' Allow me to remember that you have rescued me and called me out of darkness, setting my feet on a firm foundation. Lord, fill me and _____ with the knowledge of your will, filling us with wisdom and understanding. Generously give us your spirit so that we can live a life worthy of our calling and please you in all that we say and do. May we bear fruit, in and out of conflict, and strengthen us, giving us endurance and patience. Show us how to live out the redemption that you gave us on the cross.

humility

Ephesians 4:2

I pray that you would live a life worthy of the calling you have received. Be completely humble and gentle; be patient, bearing with one another in love. Make every effort to keep the unity of the Spirit through the bond of peace.

Father, I ask that you remind _____ of your love. Because of Jesus, you have designated both me and _____ as worthy. By your grace, you have called us to a higher way of living. You have called us to be humble, and gentle, and patient. You have called us to bear with one another in love. Give us the ability to do just that. Show us what it means to love each other. Show us how to protect our peace and unify us through your spirit. With your love in the forefront of our minds, may we both live lives worthy of the calling we have received.

unity

John 17:23

May they be brought to complete unity to let the world know that you sent me and have loved them, even as I have loved them.

Jesus, this was your prayer for your followers- unity. It is the cry of your heart as it is a way to testify to the world about your goodness! Yet unity seems so impossible right now and I don't know what that even looks like. However, you are a God who can do anything and since I know that your desire is for unity, I ask that you bring _____ and I together. Usher in reconciliation and be glorified through it. Show us both what steps we need to take in order to love one another and build a bridge to unity.

community

Ecclesiastes 4:9-10

Two are better than one, because they have a good return for their work: If one falls down, his friend can help him up, but pity the man who falls and has no one to help him up.

I recognize that you created us to live in fellowship with one another. Will you guide both _____ and I as we work through our differences? Will you protect community in both of our lives? I pray against division of any kind but ask that you would surround us both with godly community. Would you send us both wise counselors, good friends, trustworthy pastors, and others who would speak truth into our lives. Give us also the ability to discern the voices of ungodly advisors. May we reject any advice that does not line up with what you have spoken to us in your word. May our hearts be open to the influence of godly community, and may we trust your ability to provide what we each need in this season.

11

words

Ephesians 4:29-5:2

Do not let any unwholesome talk come out of your mouths, but only what is helpful for building others up according to their needs, that it may benefit those who listen. And do not grieve the Holy Spirit of God, with whom you were sealed for the day of redemption. Get rid of all bitterness, rage and anger, brawling and slander, along with every form of malice. Be kind and compassionate to one another, forgiving each other just as in Christ, God forgave you. Be imitators of God, therefore, as dearly loved children, and live a life of love, just as Christ loved us and gave himself up for us as a fragrant offering and sacrifice to God.

Lord God, as we work through this conflict, would you guard my mouth and the mouth of _____. Keep us from saying anything unpleasing to you. Give us both words that will bless and not destroy, words that will build up and not tear down. May our words not grieve you. I ask that you remove all arguing and slander from our talk. Instead, would you replace these destructive words with kindness, compassion, and give us the ability to forgive each other. Help _____ and I to follow you, living in your example of love, even in the way we speak. May we lay ourselves down to lift you up.

12

freedom

Galatians 5:13-16

You, my brothers and sisters, were called to be free. But do not use your freedom to indulge the flesh; rather, serve one another humbly in love. For the entire law is fulfilled in keeping this one command: "Love your neighbor as yourself." If you bite and devour each other, watch out or you will be destroyed by each other. So, I say, walk by the Spirit, and you will not gratify the desires of the flesh.

Sometimes the desires of my flesh are overwhelming. Help me, Lord Jesus, to walk by your spirit. Help _____ to walk in your spirit as well. Give both _____ and I a healthy mindset about how to use the freedom you've given us. Give us the wisdom on when to speak, and when to stay silent. Give us direction on when to act and when to be still. May we use our freedom to love, serve, and bless. Please protect us from temptation to do otherwise. Show me what this looks like and help me to use my freedom to build up and demonstrate kindness, even those who have offended me. Lord, how would you have me serve _____ in this season? Please show me what love looks like in this relationship.

13

battle for your soul

Ephesians 6:10-18

Be strong in the Lord and in his mighty power. Put on the full armor of God so that you can take your stand against the devil's schemes. For our struggle is not against flesh and blood, but against the rulers, against the authorities, against the powers of this dark world and against the spiritual forces of evil in the heavenly realms. Therefore, put on the full armor of God, so that when the day of evil comes, you may be able to stand your ground, and after you have done everything, to stand. Stand firm then, with the belt of truth buckled around your waist, with the breastplate of righteousness in place, and with your feet fitted with the readiness that comes from the gospel of peace. In addition to all this, take up the shield of faith, with which you can extinguish all the flaming arrows of the evil one. Take the helmet of salvation and the sword of the Spirit, which is the word of God. And pray in the spirit on all occasions with all kinds of prayers and request. With this in mind, be alert and always keep on praying for the saints.

Lord Jesus, there is a battle going on between _____ and me. Not only in our relationship, but also in our souls. I know the enemy desires to keep us bitter, angry, and feeling entitled, but your way is the way of peace. As _____ and I fight this battle, give us wisdom to recognize the battle happening within our hearts and minds. Prepare us Lord, and help us stand strong against these attacks, giving us the ability to seek peace. May our minds dwell only on truth. May our hearts be filled with righteousness. May we only move towards peace and not towards strife. Give us great faith and enable us to stand strong in the face of spiritual attacks. Keep us grounded in your word and allow us to constantly be filled with your spirit, discerning all that is happening. Lead us in truth and may you receive the glory for it.

14

comparison

Galatians 6:2-5

Carry each other's burdens, and in this way, you will fulfill the law of Christ. If anyone thinks they are something when they are not, they deceive themselves. Each one should test their own actions. Then they can take pride in themselves alone, without comparing themselves to someone else, for each one should carry their own load.

Father, guard my heart and the heart of _____ against comparison. Help me not to expect more of _____ than what is realistic. Give me a right mind that I would not exaggerate or minimize myself or others. Show me what my part is in this conflict and give me humility and wisdom with how to move forward. Show me how to have compassion and empathy for _____, giving me a better understanding of how _____ thinks, believes, and behaves.

15

love

1 Corinthians 13:24

Nobody should seek his own good, but the good of others. Love is patient, love is kind. It does not envy, it does not boast, it is not proud. It does not dishonor others, it is not self-seeking, it is not easily angered, it keeps no record of wrongs. Love does not delight in evil but rejoices with the truth. It always protects, always trusts, always hopes, always perseveres. Love never fails.

Father, fill _____ and I with your love. Give us hearts that love you, and hearts that love each other. Align my heart and my head so that I can love _____ in a way that is pleasing to you. Show me what kindness looks like with _____. Guard my heart against being self-seeking, keep me from anger, and help me learn to let go of what has wounded me. Protect me from doing anything that would dishonor _____ and give me ways to communicate with integrity. May both _____ and I not tolerate excuses or false pretenses, but may we rejoice in what is true. Enlarge our faith, and may we never give up hope that you can do immeasurably more than all we can ask or imagine.

16

pride

Philippians 2:3-5

Do nothing out of selfish ambition or vain conceit. Rather, in humility value others above yourselves, not looking to your own interests but each of you to the interests of the others. In your relationships with one another, have the same mindset as Christ Jesus.

God, please remove all traces of self-interest and pride from me and from _____ and clothe us with humility. It's so easy for me to get wound up in my own thoughts and ideas but help me to remember that you created _____ and that you love her/him, just like you love me. I let go of my 'right' to be right, my 'right' to an apology, and my 'right' to be understood. I confess that true healing comes from you, and not from any words or actions on behalf of _____. Grow an empathetic heart within me, prohibit me from saying things or doing things for selfish reasons. If there is a way for me to serve _____, please lead me in this, and give me sufficient courage to follow through.

gratitude

Colossians 3:12-15

Therefore, as God's chosen people, holy and dearly loved, clothe yourselves with compassion, kindness, humility, gentleness and patience. Bear with each other and forgive one another if any of you has a grievance against someone. Forgive as the Lord forgave you. And over all these virtues put on love, which binds them all together in perfect unity. Let the peace of Christ rule in your hearts, since as members of one body you were called to peace. And be thankful.

Lord, you have called me chosen, holy, and loved. May my heart and mind embrace this truth, and would you help me to forgive _____. Would you also give _____ the ability to forgive me? Help us to love you and love each other, giving us hearts filled with compassion, kindness, humility, gentleness, and patience. Where I struggle, give me strength. Where I am afraid give me courage, and where I am confused, bring me clarity. No matter what I say and do to _____, may it be done out of a heart of love and not of vengeance or bitterness. Give _____ and I your peace and show us both how to walk in gratitude.

18

differences

2 Timothy 2:24

Don't have anything to do with foolish and stupid arguments, because you know they produce quarrels. And the Lord's servant must not be quarrelsome but must be kind to everyone, able to teach, not resentful.

Father, as _____ and I work through our differences, would you guard our hearts against foolish and stupid arguments? Would you enable us to get to the heart of the issue and not get distracted with surface problems? Help us learn to communicate with gentleness and respect and help us to avoid quarreling as I know this does not honor you. In the midst of conflict, show me how to handle myself in a way that is pleasing to you, and help me to not hold on to any resentments. I release _____ to you, give me a forgiving heart.

19

empathy

1 Peter 3:8-9

Finally, all of you, be like-minded, be sympathetic, love one another, be compassionate and humble. Do not repay evil with evil or insult with insult. On the contrary, repay evil with blessing, because to this you were called so that you may inherit a blessing.

God, in the midst of this strife, help me to be sympathetic. Help me to remember the humanity of my offender and how she/he needs grace, just like I do. Give _____ and I the ability to be understanding of one another. Show us what love looks like in this conflict and help us to act with compassion and humility. Speak to me right now about ways I can show compassion to _____. Fill me with your spirit that I might not react to insults and hurtful actions in a way that would further damage the relationship. Help me to lay down ongoing offenses and forgive so that my heart would be blameless before you. By your grace, keep me from further hurting _____. Help me to always take the high road, and help me to not hurt others, just because I've been hurt. Help me to understand how _____ might be feeling and fill my heart with compassion. Give me the ability to bless and love those who have hurt me.

20

do good

Galatians 6:9-10

Let us not become weary in doing good, for at the proper time we will reap a harvest if we do not give up. Therefore, as we have opportunity, let us do good to all people, especially to those who belong to the family of believers.

Lord, I am weary. This conflict exhausts me, and I am tired from carrying this burden. Come alongside me and help me to not give up and not give in. Help me to have hope in the future, and may I not give up on believing in you. May I not give up on _____. Open my eyes to the ways _____ may be trying to do good to me. You've commanded us to do good 'to all people,' which includes _____. Will you give me a fresh vision for what doing good to _____ might look like? Release me from my own expectations and the expectations of others so that I can do the good you are calling me to do and give me courage to act quickly on what you've asked me to do.

21

blessing

Numbers 6:24-26

The Lord bless you and keep you; the Lord make his face to shine upon you and be gracious to you; the Lord turn his face to you and give you peace.

Lord Jesus, would you bless _____ and draw her/him close to you. Would you shine your face upon her/him and would you be gracious to her/him. Let your peace rest upon her/him. May _____ be awed at your presence today and would you do great things in her/his life. Pour out your spirit on _____ and allow them to experience you in new and powerful ways. I pray that you would heal the places in _____'s heart that need healing. I pray that you would be _____'s provider and comforter in times of trouble. I pray that you would lead and guide _____ in the ways of Jesus and lead them to green pastures and still waters. I pray that you would allow _____ to live in their God-given identity and that they would bring you glory all of their days.

Amen.

ABOUT THE AUTHOR

Crystal McGowen

AUTHOR | COUNSELOR | SPEAKER | COACH

www.CrystalMcGowen.com

Crystal is a non-clinical, Christian counselor and Soul Care provider based in Portland, Oregon. She helps women better understand how God is working in their lives, and equips them to tell their stories. Crystal serves women around the world by equipping them to take steps towards forgiveness, emotional health, and spiritual maturity. She offers online counseling, coaching, and soul care appointments to help women grow closer to Jesus.

You can follow Crystal on Instagram @Crystal.McGowen.Counselor or go to her website and subscribe to her monthly newsletter.

Are we called to forgive and forget?

Forgive and forget.

I think we've all heard it, and I think we've all suffered because of it. In fact, this one little phrase caused years of doubt and pain in my life. My offender repeatedly told me that "If I would just forgive, forget, and move on," then everything would be fine. And I wondered… is that what it takes? Is my emotional and spiritual well-being directly tied to my ability to forgive and forget?

If that's what it took to be fine, I was committed. But, something about the process didn't sit right with me. I knew that I was called to forgive, but the forgetting part never made sense to me.

How could I actually forget what was said and done?
Is it even possible?
What if I can't forget?
Is my ability to forgive limited by my memories?

I couldn't find the answers to my questions, and I found myself confused and frustrated. Erasing the painful memories in my heart did not seem very doable or practical, and I know that I am not alone in this struggle. Many women are confused with what forgiveness really means, and because we've heard this little phrase, 'forgive and forget' all our lives, we start to erroneously equate forgiving with forgetting.

Memories are interesting, aren't they? I find there are two main approaches to our memories. People either block them out because they are so painful, or they have trouble dwelling on much else.

If forgetting and blocking out painful memories is your default, I encourage you to allow Jesus to heal your memories. We have a good teacher who has told us that the truth sets us free (John 8:32). I strongly encourage you to speak with a trusted friend, pastor, counselor, or other helping professional who can help you process the memories that you've blocked out. Allowing yourself to experience healing from the locked doors of your heart is important to lasting emotional and spiritual health.

However, for those of you who find yourself overwhelmed and mentally consumed by your painful memories, there's a chance the 'forgive and forget' mentality might make you feel guilty for not being able to let go.

This was my story, and after having studied and prayed through this issue, I want to share something with you, *you don't have to forget in order to forgive.*

Go ahead, re-read that a few times if you need to.

Breathe it in and let that truth start healing your heart.

You are not called to forget.

You are called to forgive.

Because so many of us grew up believing the 'forgive and forget' line, the statement above might make some feel a bit uncomfortable, but stay with me. I'd love to share with you why your memories are important, both psychologically, and spiritually.

THE PSYCHOLOGICAL EXPLANATION

Just the other day I was cooking with my daughter, who is almost 8. Even though we've cooked together many times before, for some reason as soon as I took the pan off of the burner, she decided to put her sweet little finger on the glowing red stovetop. She very quickly withdrew her blistered finger, and ice was applied as we revisited kitchen safety.

As this is the first time she's experienced the pain of a hot stove, I'm counting on this lesson sticking with her, providing her with a memory that will protect her from future accidents. As a mother, I want my children to remember that burns hurt, and to smartly avoid them. I want them to grow from their painful experiences, not deny them. It would not serve my daughter well to 'forget' about the painful burn.

> The same is true of our memories. Our memories serve to protect us against potential painful situations in the future.

Forgetting in some situations is actually dangerous and can lead to greater harm. When you've been hurt, forgetting makes you more vulnerable. It doesn't protect you or serve you when you deny what has happened.

If you have experienced a soul wound - the kind of wound that demands a response and changes you, it's not really possible to forget what's happened. How could you? The concept is completely unrealistic. Forgiveness doesn't bring about amnesia, after all.

So why do we put pressure on ourselves to forget what has happened? Forgiveness doesn't cause us to forget, but it does cause us to remember things differently. Let me explain.

A person who has forgiven is able to share their story, their heartache and pain without the bitterness or resentment. The events in their past remain the same, but their attitude has changed. The way they view their offender has changed, and they are able to view their past through a lens of grace.

When you choose to forgive, you are not erasing memories. You are not forgetting what hurt you, or who hurt you, but instead you are healing your heart and mind.

Psychologically speaking, to forget is impossible and impractical, and can even be detrimental.

THE SPIRITUAL EXPLANATION

I want you to think back at a time when you heard an amazing testimony. You know, the kind that leaves you completely amazed at the brilliance and generosity of God. The kind where you're awestruck, humbled, excited, and the whole story just wants to make you get down on your knees in a blubbering mess and praise God! Think back on that story for a moment.

What makes it so beautiful?
Why is it so powerful?

Chances are, the story was so moving because through their testimony, you were able to hear the before and after. They probably shared the hardship, the dysfunction, the abuse and seemingly impossible circumstances, only to be rescued, redeemed, and redefined by an all-loving God. The mess is what makes the testimony so beautiful.

Can you imagine the same testimony if the speaker had 'forgotten' all the mess? If they had forgotten where they came from? If they had forgotten who they were before Jesus?

It is our transformed lives and our testimonies that help show others who Jesus is.

When we share our hardships in light of God's abundance, the lives of others are changed, and God is glorified. Consider this testimony of Paul:

> I've worked much harder, been jailed more often, beaten up more times than I can count, and at death's door time after time. I've been flogged five times with the Jews' thirty-nine lashes, beaten by Roman rods three times, pummeled with rocks once. I've been shipwrecked three times, and immersed in the open sea for a night and a day. In hard travelling year in and year out, I've had to ford rivers, fend off robbers, struggle with friends, struggle with foes. I've been at risk in the city, at risk in the country, endangered by desert sun and sea storm, and betrayed by those I thought were my

brothers. I've known drudgery and hard labor, many a long and lonely night without sleep, many a missed meal, blasted by the cold, naked to the weather.

And that's not the half of it, when you throw in the daily pressures and anxieties of all the churches. When someone gets to the end of his rope, I feel the desperation in my bones. When someone is duped into sin, an angry fire burns in my gut.

If I have to "brag" about myself, I'll brag about the humiliations that make me like Jesus.

2 Corinthians 11:24-30, (The Message)

We see no 'forgetting' with Paul. In fact, had he forgotten, his testimony wouldn't be nearly as compelling. Let me challenge you with something.

The pain in your past gives you validity and authority to speak
the truth to a lost and broken world.

The reason Paul's life is so amazing is because we can see the before and after. Clearly, Paul's difficult, painful memories are still intact, yet he uses them to point others to Jesus. He doesn't deny them or excuse them, but he shares them to show the power of God. As a result, the world is changed. My friend, this powerful calling isn't limited to Paul. God will use your story to bring healing to others who are questioning, confused, and broken.

For the sake of the Kingdom, don't deny your painful past, but
through the power of forgiveness, let God use those wounds for
His glory and His purposes.

Let's tackle one more common argument before we finish. If you've grown up in the church or been in the church for very long, you may have heard Philippians 3:13 referenced regarding forgiveness:

Forgetting what is behind and straining toward what is ahead, I press on toward the goal to win the prize for which God has called me heavenward in Christ Jesus.

This is a beautiful passage and one that we should absolutely be living out, but if you dig in deeper, you will find that the word 'forget' doesn't exactly translate in the way you think it would.

Ἐπιλανθάνομαι is the Greek word used for forget here, and when translated is read "forgetting, neglecting, or no longer caring for (Strong's Number G1950)."

So, if we were to rephrase this verse according to the original Greek meaning, it might sound something like, "Don't keep glancing back at the past, but keep your eyes focused on the future." In the context of forgiveness, this makes sense.

We can acknowledge our past without being fixated on it. If Paul had chosen to constantly look over his shoulder at all the mess that he had caused, and all the mess that others had caused him, he wouldn't have been able to run freely toward the goal.

Here's the challenge: *don't deny your past, but don't dwell on it either.* Your past is your past, it is what it is. BUT- it doesn't define you unless you let it. If you keep your eyes focused on the Kingdom, like Paul did, you can run the race with endurance, passion, and purpose.

As a soul care provider, I find that usually our greatest pain points in life are rooted in unforgiveness. Learning to forgive is a complicated, yet rewarding journey, and if you'd like encouragement, accountability, and support, I offer online forgiveness coaching to equip you to take the next step.

For more information, please go to
www.CrystalMcGowen.com

CLOSING PRAYER

Lord give me…
Contentment when I am wanting,
Peace when I am striving,
Patience when I am waiting,
Comfort when I am crying,
Joy when I am hurting,
Hope when I am denying,
Faith when I am doubting,
Words when I am speaking,
Encouragement when I am wavering,
And blessing when I am following.

Bless you,

Crystal McGowen

Made in the USA
Columbia, SC
21 March 2019